A Field Guide to Common Plants

of the Santa Barbara Foothills and Southern California

by Hugh Margerum and David Powdrell

**A Field Guide to Common Plants
of the Santa Barbara Foothills and Southern California**

By Hugh Margerum and David Powdrell

Cismontane Publishing
5290 Overpass Road, Suite 227
Santa Barbara, California   93111 USA

First Printing 2005
Printed in Hong Kong

ISBN 0-9754048-0-6

TABLE OF CONTENTS

Santa Barbara is a magical place. Full of striking Spanish architecture, bordering the beautiful Pacific Ocean and set against colorful foothills that provide a lush backdrop to our area, we are constantly reminded that our city is a treasure.

Hugh Margerum and David Powdrell have done a wonderful job of capturing a bit of the magic of Santa Barbara in this book, *A Field Guide to Common Plants of the Santa Barbara Foothills and Southern California*. Their research at the Botanic Gardens combined with the captivating photographs give the reader a glimpse at the wonderful world of botany just outside our back door.

Enjoy the read, but more importantly; follow their lead. Put on your walking shoes and saunter up the foothills to enjoy some of the most spectacular views in the world. You'll certainly come across many of the plants and wildflowers outlined in this book, and you'll learn a bit of their history, and some of their nutritional, and medicinal uses too.

Mayor Marty Blum

INTRODUCTION

The Mediterranean climate of southern California is home to an amazing variety of interesting, useful, and colorful plantlife—both native and introduced. The Native American Chumash, who lived for thousands of years on the Central Coast, depended on many of the native plants, for food, medicine, tools, and basketry.

During our weekly hikes up and down the trails of Santa Barbara's foothills, the idea occurred to us that we might try to identify at least some of the myriad plant varieties we encountered. The several guides we consulted, while helpful, were either not specific enough to the area, were too scientific for novices such as ourselves, or were simply too vast for our needs. We decided to photograph and identify plants and make a simple little book for our own use and possibly give to friends and family. So, after many more hikes—(with cameras and notebooks in hand), meetings with experts, consulting local libraries, researching on and offline—this field guide came together as a slightly expanded version of the original idea. Our intention is to provide a simple lay-person's field guide to the flora of the area with the hope that knowledge increases appreciation and understanding both of the plants and the habitat in which they grow.

The scope of this book is intentionally limited; only the more common or noteworthy plants have been included and are described in simple terms. While we try to avoid words such as *anceolate*, *glabrous*, *strigose*, *papilionaceous*, and *subulate* in our descriptions, two terms we came across are important to know and contribute to understanding the plants and habitat we cover in this book and are defined below:

Chaparral – The collection of woody plants that make up the majority of the brushy covering of the foothills.

Cismontane – The ocean facing side of the coastal range, which is generally as far as we ventured in photographing the flora in this book.

For further study please see some of the resources listed in the bibliography, and especially make use of the Santa Barbara Botanic Garden's wonderful educational facilities.

–Hugh Margerum and David Powdrell

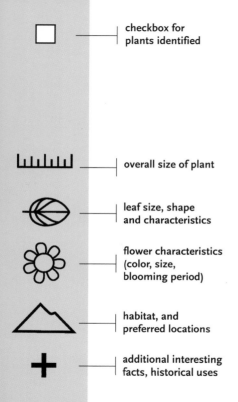

checkbox for
plants identified

overall size of plant

leaf size, shape
and characteristics

flower characteristics
(color, size,
blooming period)

habitat, and
preferred locations

additional interesting
facts, historical uses

How to use this book

The sections of this book are organized by color of each plant's flowers with the last section containing non-blooming plants or plants with insignificant flowers.

Note that most of the photos were taken in the springtime when the plants are at their most luxuriant and in full bloom. More investigation may be required to ID a plant whose leaves have dropped or changed color and/or are not flowering.

The pages are laid out with basic details so each plant can be identified quickly and easily.

We were surprised to learn that much of the flora is made up of non-native plants (such as the ubiquitous Black Mustard). Many have made themselves at home in the foothills and along roadsides; some are considered invasive pests. We have noted in boldface if a plant is a native or non-native in the plant description.

For links and more information or to contact the authors, please visit our website at: **www.sbplants.com**

A note on edible plants: *Please be aware that while many plants and flowers in our area are edible, others are poisonous to the point to being deadly. Further, what may resemble an edible plant pictured and described here may actually be a poisonous look-alike. The Chumash Indians and other tribes learned over decades and centuries what was safe to eat what wasn't. Please do your own research fully and carefully, and be sure to consult an expert before eating any wild plant.*

ACKNOWLEDGEMENTS

We are indebted to the Santa Barbara Botanic Garden, in particular the following staff members: Laurie Hannah, Librarian, for her advice and expert proof-reading, and to Barry Tanowitz, Director of Science Education, and Dieter H. Wilken, Vice President of Programs and Collections for invaluable help in identifying the plants in this book.

All photographs by the authors.

Bigberry Manzanita

Species: Arctostaphylos glauca
Family: Ericaceae (Heath family)

Deep reddish-brown bark distinguishes this small **native** tree, which grows to twenty-five feet tall.

This manzanita's leaves are grayish green, rounded, non-serrated and up to 3" long.

White, unusual tiny bell-shaped flowers bloom from December to March.

This small tree thrives in the coastal sage environment.

Manzanita means "little apple" in Spanish.
The berries make a great jelly.

Blue Elderberry

Species: Sambucus mexicana
Family: Caprifoliaceae (Honeysuckle family)

A **native** shrub-tree, the Blue Elderberry grows to twenty-feet tall.

The leaves are serrated and oval with pointed tips and are up to 6" long.

Tiny individual white flowers with 5 petals mass in 8" clusters, and bloom from April to August.

A drought tolerant shrub, it is common in the canyons and valleys of the Santa Barbara hills.

The berries make great jams, jellies, pies and wines. If not cooked properly they can be toxic!

California Blackberry

Species: Rubus ursinus
Family: Rosaceae (Rose family)

Vines of the **native** wild blackberry grow to over thirty feet in length.

The leaves are very jaggedy with spiny hair-like growth. They measure up to 6" long.

The white flowers are approximately 1" across with five petals and a yellow center.

Blackberries grow best in sunny, hot climates of the foothills.

Black when ripe, the edible berries are found in late summer and fall.

California Sagebrush

Species: Artemisia californica
Family: Asteraceae (Sunflower family)

Sometimes called "cowboy cologne", the **native** California Sagebrush grows to five feet tall.

Soft evergrey 1" - 2" long needle-like leaves grow from the soft branches of the sagebrush.

Miniscule white flowers bloom from August to February.

A dominant plant of the chaparral, it thrives in the coastal ranges.

Native Americans made tea from the stems, which helped reduce fevers. Despite the name, it is not a true sage.

Chamise

Species: Adenostoma fasciculatum
Family: Rosaceae (Rose family)

A hearty **native** shrub, the Chamise is a main component of the chaparral, growing to ten feet tall.

The tiny resinous leaves are stiff and linear to 3/8" and clustered on short shoots.

Tiny white flower clusters bloom in late spring.

Chamise is a drought tolerant plant common among the coastal chaparral.

Native Americans used Chamise wood for arrow shafts.

Coyote Brush

Species: Baccharis pilularis
Family: Asteraceae (Sunflower family)

This **native** California evergreen plant grows to
twelve feet tall.

Its light green leaves are up to 1 1/2" long, oval,
and alternate on the branches.

Small white clustered flowers bloom from August through
December, followed by tiny fruit with a dramatic fluffy
covering.

This plant is very common in the coastal sage
scrub of the Santa Barbara foothills.

Thought to have been used by the Chumash as an
antidote for poison oak. Also useful as a landscape plant.

Dodder

Species: Cuscuta californica
Family: Convolvulaceae (Morning glory family)

This most unusual **native** parasitic weed grows into a yellow-orange stringy mat.

The Dodder is a leafless plant.

It generates very tiny 1/8" white flower clusters that bloom in the spring.

Not common, but occasional mats of Dodder inhabit the Santa Barbara foothills.

This parasite attaches itself to another plant and sucks nutrients and water from the host.

Greenspot Nightshade

Species: Solanum douglasii
Family: Solanaceae (Nightshade family)

Also known as White Nightshade, this poisonous **native** perennial shrub grows to six feet tall.

The leaves are dark green in color and up to 4" long with pointed tips.

The tiny white flowers have a yellow center and bloom in the spring, followed by small green to black berries.

Found on most every trail, it grows most abundantly in partial sun environment.

The entire Greenspot Nightshade plant is poisonous to humans.

Laurel Sumac

Species: Malosma laurina
Family: Anacardiaceae (Sumac family)

A large, rounded evergreen shrub, this **native** component of the chaparral grows to fifteen feet tall.

Its leaves, up to 4" long, are reddish, leathery, and folded along a central vein.

Tiny white flowers in dense clusters bloom in June and July.

The Laurel Sumac grows on dry ridges and canyons below 3000' elevation.

Susceptible to frost, it was planted by citrus growers as a frost indicator.

Miner's Lettuce

Species: Claytonia perfoliata
Family: Portulacaceae (Purslane family)

A small leafy clustered green plant that grows to one foot tall.

Round, dark green leaves, 3 - 4" diameter.

A tiny white flower and stalk emerges from center of the leaf from February through May.

It is common in moist, often shady places below 5000' elevation.

It was eaten by California gold rush miners to fight scurvy.

Morning Glory

Species: Calystegia macrostegia
Family: Convolvulaceae (Morning glory family)

A creeping **native** vine, Morning Glory grows to two feet tall.

Its light green triangular leaves measure up to 4" in length.

Attractive white flowers bloom from April through September.

This plant is found in fields and open spaces below 5000' elevation.

Despised by many as an obnoxious weed in gardens and orchards.

Poison Oak

Species: Toxicodendron diversilobum
Family: Anacardiaceae (Sumac family)

Poison Oak is a **native** climbing vine or shrub abundant in the foothills of Santa Barbara.

Poison Oak leaves can be multi-colored and usually alternate on the stems in groups of three leaflets.

In late spring, small greenish-white flowers are produced in the leaf axils.

One of the more abundant plants in the foothills, it grows at elevations below 5000'.

The twigs as well as the leaves contain urushiol oil, which causes the dreaded rash to those susceptible. Best avoided.

Sticky Snakeroot

Species: Ageratina adenophora
Family: Asteraceae (Sunflower family)

This **non-native** plant grows to six feet tall.

Sticky Snakeroot has large green, pointed leaves with serrated edges.

The flowers are white, pincushion-like, grow in clusters and bloom April through July.

It needs plenty of shade and moist soil to flourish and is usually found near creeks.

This plant is a highly invasive, non-native weed.

Toyon

Species: Heteromeles arbutifolia
Family: Rosaceae (Rose family)

This **native** evergreen shrub grows to twenty-five feet tall.

The finely toothed leaves grow to 4" long and are glossy green.

Small white flowers in terminal clusters bloom in the spring. Dramatic red berries adorn the plants in winter months.

It's a common plant on the dry chaparral slopes of the foothills.

The Chumash roasted the berries over open coals or boiled them in baskets.

Wild Mint

Species: Mentha arvensis
Family: Lamiaceae (Mint family)

This familiar **native** plant grows along streambeds
to two feet tall.

Wild Mint leaves are ovate or wedge shaped at the base
and hairy on both sides.

Tiny clustered white, violet or pink flowers bloom from July
to October

Wild Mint is found in or near streambeds of the Santa Barbara
foothills.

This plant has both nutritional and medicinal properties
and a recognizable mint fragrance.

Black Mustard

Species: Brassica nigra
Family: Brassicaceae (Mustard family)

A fast growing annual herb, this **non-native** plant grows to ten feet tall.

The tiny lower leaves are flat and divided; the upper leaves are oblong.

Small yellow flowers cluster at the ends of the thin stems. It flowers from May through June.

Abundant in the Santa Barbara foothills; it adapts to many California climates.

It is naturalized from Europe, but was supposedly introduced here by the Franciscan Padres who scattered the seed along the Camino Real to mark the route.

Yucca

Species: Yucca whipplei
Family: Agavaceae (Agave family)

This **native** plant sends long erect flower shoots from a spiny base that can be up to six feet across.

Large, three-foot long, gray-green, narrow spine-tipped leaves form the base of this plant.

Masses of white or cream flowers bloom April through May on a stalk up to eleven feet tall.

The Yucca thrives on stony slopes in chaparral at elevations below 4000'.

Chumash Indians made flour from the seeds and soap from the roots. The plants die after flowering.

Bush Monkey Flower

Species: Mimulus aurantiacus
Family: Scrophulariaceae (Figwort family)

This **native** showy shrub grows to four feet tall.

Bush Monkey Flower leaves are 1" - 3" long, narrow, and are sticky to the touch.

The distinctively shaped yellow to orange flowers bloom March through August.

Most typically found in soft chaparral, particularly after a fire.

The stigma lips will close if poked with a twig, protecting the pollen within.

Bush Poppy

Species: Dendromecon rigida
Family: Papaveraceae (Poppy family)

An erect, slender-stemmed **native**, this perennial shrub grows to ten feet tall.

The leaves are grey-green in color, oblong in shape, and up to 4" long.

The bright yellow four-petalled flowers bloom from March through June.

This plant prefers a dry stony wash in elevations up to 5000'.

This plant thrives after a fire has moved through the area.

California Bay Laurel

Species: Umbellularia californica
Family: Lauraceae (Laurel family)

This mighty, **native** tree grows to over one hundred feet tall, though it is often seen as a shrub.

Leaves of the California Bay Laurel are dark green, pointed, aromatic and 2" - 4" long.

Tiny yellow flowers bloom from March through June.

It's common in the chaparral environment in canyons and valleys below 5000'.

Chumash used the leaves as a flea repellant and also to make a tea to treat headaches and stomach distress. It can be used as a flavor in cooking.

Canyon Sunflower

Species: Venegasia carpesioides
Family: Asteraceae (Sunflower family)

A **native**, perennial shrub, the Canyon Sunflower grows to five feet tall.

Its leaves are 2"- 4" long, bright green, and heart-shaped with jagged edges and fine hairs.

Large vibrant yellow flowers bloom February through September.

This plant is found in the cool shaded canyons of the Santa Barbara foothills.

The botanic name *Venegasia* remembers Padre Miguel Venegas (1680-1764), a Jesuit scholar and historian at a seminary in Puebla, Mexico.

Fennel

Species: Foeniculum vulgare
Family: Apiaceae (Parsley family)

An erect plant with polished green stems, this **non-native** exceeds six feet in height.

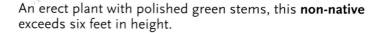

Fennel leaves are wispy green and have a strong licorice aroma.

Yellow, carrot-top like flowers bloom in July and August.

It grows abundantly in most soil conditions of the coastal chaparral.

Fennel has numerous culinary and medicinal uses; the root bulb is used in many Italian dishes.

Golden Yarrow

Species: Eriophyllum confertiflorum
Family: Asteraceae (Sunflower family)

This abundant **native** perennial shrub grows to two feet tall.

The small, slender, erect leaves alternate on the stems.

Yellow flowers clustered at the top of upright stems bloom March through August.

Common on many trails, this plant thrives in the Santa Barbara chaparral.

Folklore claims that the yarrow species was used as a blood coagulant among early American colonists.

Mugwort

Species: Artemisia douglasiana
Family: Asteraceae (Sunflower family)

A **native** perennial herb, Mugwort grows to six feet tall.

Jagged grey-green leaves with silver undersides characterize this plant.

This medicinal herb has pale yellow to reddish flowers and blooms from June through October.

Found most commonly in open to shady areas to 6000' elevation.

This relative of Wormwood (the source of absinthe) has had many medicinal and nutritional uses throughout history.

Prickly Pear Cactus

Species: Opuntia littoralis
Family: Cactaceae (Cactus family)

The **native** Prickly Pear Cactus grows to over seven feet tall.

The cactus has fleshy, spiny pads instead of leaves, which are used by the plant for storing water.

Large red, purple, or yellow flowers bloom in the spring.

The cactus likes a dry, hot, desert-like climate.

Pear-shaped fruit are edible, as are the pads, *nopalitos* of Mexican cuisine.

Spanish Broom

Species: Spartium junceum
Family: Fabaceae (Pea family)

A perennial **non-native** evergreen broom, this invasive plant grows to ten feet tall.

The Broom's erect, bright green stems are rounded (rush-like) and mainly leafless.

The bright yellow fragrant flowers bloom May through August.

This plant is drought resistant and loves full sun.
It can grow in poor rocky soil.

In earlier times, the bundled stems were used to make brooms.

Tree Tobacco

Species: Nicotiana glauca
Family: Solanaceae (Nightshade family)

This common **non-native** plant grows to fifteen feet tall in the Santa Barbara foothills.

Its leaves grow to 6" long, are light or grayish green and have a thin waxy coating.

The long, tubular, clustered yellow flowers bloom year-round in warm climates.

A very common plant in southern California; it grows abundantly along roadsides.

All parts of the Tree Tobacco are poisonous to humans.

Virgin's Bower

Species: Clematis lasiantha
Family: Ranunculaceae (Buttercup family)

A **native** woody vine that grows to thirty or more feet, often covering chaparral shrubs.

Compound leaves with three to five leaflets are opposite on the stems.

Creamy yellow tassled flowers cover the vines from February to May.

Often found in canyons along streams and moist places.

Early California Spanish shepards called it "Yerba de Chibato" (herb of the young kid), for its use as a healing wash for the wounds of their animals.

California Poppy

Species: Eschecholzia californica
Family: Papaveraceae (Poppy family)

An upright, compact **native** plant that grows to 18" tall.

The poppy has a carrot-top like leaf pattern which is silvery green in color.

Delicate bright orange flowers blossom in profusion throughout the spring.

This drought tolerant plant grows abundantly in the arid environments of California.

Poppy flowers close up at night and on cloudy days. It is California's official state flower.

Deerweed

Species: Lotus scoparius
Family: Fabaceae (Pea family)

A California **native** plant, this small showy bush-shrub grows to four feet tall.

Deerweed leaves are tiny, narrow, and green on a stiff, brush-like stem.

Yellow, orange and red popcorn-like flowers about 1/2" long bloom year round.

Deerweed is prevalent in the foothills and is among the first plants to return to the habitat after a fire.

Deerweed has a unique ability to enrich the soil with nitrogen.

Humboldt Lily

Species: Lilium humboldtii
Family: Liliaceae (Lily family)

This most elusive **native** plant grows to over eight feet tall.

The leaves are deep green and widely spaced on stem-like trunk.

Large exotic bloom; orange with leopard-like spots.
It blooms in May and June.

Not common; it can be found in shaded areas near creeks.

The California Native Plant Society lists this plant as rare.

Climbing Penstemon

Species: Keckiella cordifolia
Family: Scrophulariaceae (Figwort family)

The Climbing Penstemon is a sprawling **native** evergreen perennial that grows to six feet.

Its leaves are small, heart-shaped, glossy-green and opposite on a viney stem.

Bright red tubular 2" flowers adorn the branches May through July.

It's usually found on north facing slopes or under shade.

This plant is a favorite for hummingbirds.

Fuchsia-Flowered Gooseberry

Species: Ribes speciosum
Family: Grossulariaceae (Gooseberry family)

This **native** evergreen shrub grows to six feet in height.

Dark green on top, the lobed leaves are 1" long, roundish with serrated edges. The branches are spine covered.

Deep ruby red flowers with tiny hair-like spines bloom in the springtime.

The Gooseberry grows best in shaded canyons and woodlands.

Found only in California and just outside state lines.

Hummingbird Sage

Species: Salvia spathacea
Family: Lamiaceae (Mint family)

This **native** medicinal sage sends pink shoots up to three feet tall.

Large, deep green, oblong, and fragrant leaves have a slightly wrinkled surface.

Magenta flowers approximately 1" long cluster on the stem and bloom from March to May.

A very common plant, found in lower elevations in full sun to partial shade.

The Latin name, salvia, means "I am well." This plant has many healing properties.

Indian Paintbrush

Species: Castilleja affinis
Family: Scrophulariaceae (Figwort family)

This showy **native** plant stands erect with red shoots that grow to two feet tall.

Its leaves are green and linear and grow to 2" long.

Vibrant red 1" long brush-like flowers bloom from March through June.

The Indian Paintbrush grows on dry brushy slopes to 4500' elevation.

Its roots are parasitic on the roots of other plants.
It is the state flower of Wyoming.

Indian Pink

Species: Silene californica
Family: Caryophyllaceae (Pink family)

A **native** soft-stemmed perennial, Indian Pink grows to three feet tall.

Indian Pink leaves grow opposite each other, are pointed and grow to 4" long.

Delicate many-tipped 1" red flowers bloom from May through July.

This plant is found on grassy slopes and shaded areas below 5000' elevation.

It is a favorite of hummingbirds.

California Wild Rose

Species: Rosa californica
Family: Rosaceae (Rose family)

This easily recognized **native** shrub grows to ten feet tall.

Wild Rose leaves are dark green and oval with many points.

Soft pink fragrant flowers bloom in the spring.

The California Rose is typically found on the coastal ranges at elevations up to 6000'.

The rose hips are high in vitamin C, and make a good quality tea. The Chumash had many uses for this plant.

Chalk Live-Forever

Species: Dudleya pulverulenta
Family: Crassulaceae (Stonecrop family)

This **native** plant has a rosette base that shoots off several two foot spikes.

Chalk Live-Forever leaves are pale green, chalky, and succulent.

Pinkish, reddish flowers that look almost other-worldly blossom May through July.

Typically found along dry, rocky slopes of the foothills at elevations below 3500'.

The base of this plant exudes a waxy secretion that helps the plant to retain moisture.

Chaparral Pea

Species: Pinkeringia montana
Family: Fabaceae (Pea family)

This **native** evergreen shrub will grow to three feet tall and six feet wide.

Chaparral Pea leaves are on spine tipped branchlets, usually 2" to 6" long.

Beautiful pink flowers bloom May through June.

This plant likes the mediterranean climate: a wet mild winter and dry hot summer.

This plant is a favorite food source for deer.

Cheeseweed

Species: Malva parviflora
Family: Malvaceae (Hibiscus family)

This common **non-native** annual grows to five feet tall.

The leaves of this plant are roundish with wavy, shallow toothed margins to 4" across.

The pinkish of bluish tinged white flowers bloom most of the year.

This plant grows in disturbed areas, fields, and orchards throughout California.

The circular fruit is about 1/2" across and resembles a minature wheel of cheese.

Lemonade Berry

Species: Rhus integrifolia
Family: Anacardiaceae (Sumac family)

A California **native**, this large, rounded evergreen shrub grows to ten feet tall.

The leathery leaves are 1" - 2" long, oval shaped, and alternate on the branches.

Small pink to white clustered flowers bloom February through May.

Lemonade Berry is found on ocean-facing slopes below 2600' elevation.

Mixed with water, the tangy berries can make a somewhat bitter lemonade-like drink.

Rose Snapdragon

Species: Antirrhinum multiflorum
Family: Scrophulariaceae (Figwort family)

Tall broom-like stems characterize this **native** plant which grows to five feet tall.

Rose Snapdragon leaves are tiny nodular outgrowths from the erect stem.

Beautiful pink and yellow flowers with soft hair-like fibers bloom from May to July.

Somewhat elusive, it grows in the chaparral at elevations below 4000'.

The snapdragon is extremely sensitive to gravity. It is geotropic, which means that when a flower is held in a horizontal position, it quickly turns upward.

Trailing Snowberry

Species: Symphoricarpos mollis
Family: Caprifoliaceae (Honeysuckle family)

The Trailing Snowberry is a **native** plant that exceeds four feet in height.

The leaves are almost perfectly round measuring 1" in diameter.

Soft pink or white flowers bloom in early spring, followed by tiny white berries.

The Trailing Snowberry prefers lots of shade and is found at elevations below 6000'.

Traditionally, Native Americans crushed the leaves of trailing snowberry to treat sores and wounds. The bark was boiled to remedy tuberculosis and venereal disease.

Blue Dicks

Species: Dichelostemma capitatum
Family: Amaryllidaceae (Amaryllis family)

This slender, long stemmed **native** plant sprouts to two feet tall.

Grasslike leaves sprout from a fibrous bulb sending up a long narrow stem.

Violet-blue clustered 1" - 2" flowers at the top of the stalk bloom from March to May.

A common plant along the Pacific coast at elevations up to 7000'.

The edible bulbs (corms) were a favorite among Native Americans.

Fiesta Flower

Species: Pholistoma auritum
Family: Hydrophyllaceae (Waterleaf family)

A prickly California **native** plant, the Fiesta Flower grows to three feet tall.

Its leaves are light green, 2"- 6" long, oblong in shape with many lobes.

Radiant blue and purple flowers about 3" across bloom from March through June.

Somewhat elusive, it grows typically on shaded slopes and deep canyons.

Its flowers were worn by young girls during Mexican celebrations of early California.

Greenbark Ceanothus

Species: Ceanothus spinosus
Family: Rhamnaceae (Buckthorn family)

The Greenbark Ceanothus is a **native** spiny shrub that grows to ten feet tall.

Its leaves are glossy dark green, oval shaped to 2$\frac{1}{2}$" long with smooth margins.

Beautiful soft white or light blue flower clusters bloom February through May.

The Greenbark and several other species of Ceanothus are a main component of the chaparral.

The Chumash Indians used the stems for baskets, and the blossoms for soap.

Woolly Blue Curls

Species: Trichostema lanatum
Family: Lamiaceae (Mint family)

A many-branched **native** perennial, the Woolly Blue Curls grows to five feet tall.

The lime-green spear-like leaves are pungently aromatic and begin about eighteen inches up the trunk.

Showy blue, pink or whitish woolly flowers bloom from April through June.

This is a common plant on dry, sunny slopes of the foothills.

The springtime flowering stems can be hung to dry and stripped for tea.

Caterpillar Phacelia

Species: Phacelia cicutaria
Family: Hydrophyllaceae (Waterleaf famly)

A **native** of California, this erect annual grows to two feet tall.

The lobed leaves are stiff and hairy, unfolding from the stem.

White and lavender flowers uncoil from the stem in the springtime.

Mostly commonly found on dry slopes near coastal sage scrub and woodland.

The plant looks very much like a caterpillar unfolding as it blooms.

Purple Nightshade

Species: Solanum xanti
Family: Solanceae (Nightshade family)

The **native** Purple Nightshade is a woody shrub that grows to four feet tall.

Greyish green and oval, the leaves shed during drought and reappear after rains.

The deep purple flowers bloom all spring and summer.

It can be found on dry rocky slopes, road cuts, and burn areas.

All parts of this plant contain the deadly alkaloid Solanine.

Chia Sage

Species: Salvia columbariae
Family: Lamiaceae (Mint family)

Long slender stalks shoot up to two feet on this **native** California plant.

Chia Sage leaves are 4" long, growing mostly at the base and are irregularly divided.

Dense round purple balls 2" in diameter bloom March through June.

A common plant in dry, disturbed chaparral below 4000' elevation.

The nutritious seeds were used as a source of energy by the Chumash.

Farewell-to-Spring

Species: Clarkia bottae
Family: Onagraceae (Evening primrose family)

An erect-stemmed **native** annual, the Farewell-to-Spring grows to two feet tall.

Its narrow leaves alternate on the stem and grow to 2" long.

Single purple flowers with four petals bloom April through July.

This plant thrives in the lower elevations of the Santa Barbara foothills.

The Clarkia species was named for Lewis & Clark explorer, Captain William Clark.

Lupine

Species: Lupinus succulentus
Family: Fabaceae (Pea family)

This California **native** plant sends shoots up to two feet .

Lupine leaflets are arranged in groups of seven.

Sweet-pea shaped, clustered purple flowers in dense spikes bloom in late spring, followed by pea-pod fruits.

Commonly found in open or disturbed areas below 2500' elevation.

Its purple springtime displays, along with poppies, make Lupine one of California's most familiar wildflowers.

Prickly Phlox

Species: Leptodactylon californicum
Family: Polemoniaceae (Phlox family)

A showy, **native** plant, Prickly Phlox grows to three feet tall.

The leaves of this plant are up to 1/2" long and grow prickly and hairlike directly from the stem.

Its funnel-formed flowers are pink to lavender, have five petals, and bloom March through July.

Commonly found on rocky, southwest facing slopes; it loves the afternoon sun.

This plant is believed to exist only in California.

Purple Sage

Species: Salvia leucophylla
Family: Lamiaceae (Mint family)

Purple sage is a **native** evergreen shrub that grows to over three feet tall.

Purple Sage leaves are tiny, fuzzy gray, and fragrant.

Fragrant round purple flowers are stacked on a long, slender stem.

It grows abundantly on the dry hillsides of the coastal chaparral.

The Chumash used the stems as friction sticks for building fires.

Curly Dock

Species: Rumex crispus
Family: Polygonaceae (Buckwheat family)

Curly Dock is a simple stemmed **native** plant that grows to six feet tall.

Its leaves are located at the base and are long and wavy, up to ten inches long.

Tiny seed-like green flowers bloom April and May, turning reddish-brown in June.

Typically the Curly Dock is found in open areas of full sun.

Native Americans used this herb for a variety of health benefits.

Horsetail

Species: Equisetum telmateia
Family: Equisetaceae (Horsetail family)

Asparagus-like shoots grow to four feet tall on this **native** plant.

Long needle-like, grey-green stems shoot out from joints of the main stem.

No flowers come from this plant.

Horsetail is found in marshy areas, springs, and along creeks.

The Romans used horsetail to clean pots and pans. It is an indicator of a water source.

PARTS OF A FLOWER

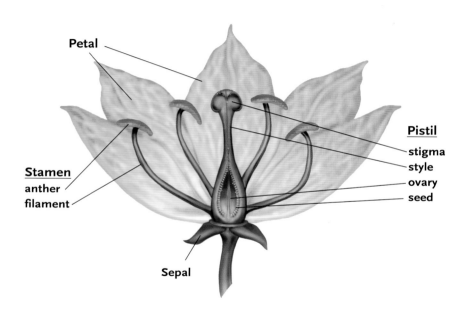

Petal

Pistil
stigma
style
ovary
seed

Stamen
anther
filament

Sepal

Index by Common Name

BIBLIOGRAPHY

Books
Abrams, Clifton, *A Flora of the Santa Barbara Region*
Abrams, Leroy, *Illustrated Flora of the Pacific States*
Belzer, Thomas J., *Roadside Plants of Southern California*
Broughton, Jacqueline, *A Sketchbook of Santa Barbara's Native Wildflowers*
Dale, Nancy, *Flowering Plants-The Santa Monica Mountains*
Heizer, R.F. and M.A. Whipple, *The California Indians-A Source Book*
Hubbard, Douglass, *Wildflowers of the Sierra*
Jepson, Willis Linn, *Manual of the Flowering Plants of California*
McAuley, Milt, *Wildflowers of the Santa Monica Mountains*
Munz, Philip A., *California Desert Wildflowers*
Rae, Cheri and John McKinney, *Walk Santa Barbara*
Robbins, W.W., Margaret Bellue and Walter Ball, *Weeds of California*
Sunset Publishing Corp., *Sunset Western Garden Book*
Walker, Phillip L. and Travis Hudson, *Chumash Healing*

Web Sites
Calflora www.calflora.org
Charters, Michael L., www.calflora.net
eNature www.enature.com
Las Pilitas Nursery www.laspilitas.com
University of California Berkeley, http://elib.cs.berkeley.edu/photos/flora/
California Native Plant Society www.cnps.org

Hugh's dog, Nellie, an arthritic ten-year old
Queensland Heeler (pictured here after rooting in a
muddy creek) accompanied us on most of our treks.

This book is dedicated to her and those of a similar bent;
always eager and ready to get out of the house and head up
into the hills for a hike!

NOTES